MENTORING THE KINGS
EMPOWERMENT THROUGH MENTORSHIP

MOSES & SIMS

GRACE FELLOWSHIP PUBLISHING @ WWW.GFPLLCUSA.COM

Copyright

First published by Grace Fellowship Publishing LLC 2024
Copyright © 2024 by Moses and Sims
All rights reserved. No part of this publication may be reproduced, stored or transmitted in any form or by any means, electronic, mechanical, photocopying, recording,

scanning, or otherwise without written permission from the publisher. It is illegal to copy this book, post it to a website, or distribute it by any other means without permission.

Moses and Sims asserts the moral right to be identified as the author of this work. Moses and Sims has no responsibility for the persistence or accuracy of URLs for external or third-party Internet Websites referred to in this publication and does not guarantee that any content on such Websites is, or will remain, accurate or appropriate.
First edition

Advisor: Godwin Moses
Cover art by Jo Anne Sims
Editing by Megan Blash

Epigragh

These words of wisdom have been crafted to inspire encouragement, foster growth, and empower you with effective strategies to mentor yourself—the king within.

Contents

Foreword
Preface

Acknowlegement
Introduction

Part One
The Descent and Awakening

CHAPTER 1 2
The Fall

CHAPTER 2 7
Meeting Marcus

CHAPTER 3 13
Re-framing the Past

Part Two
Foundations of Change

CHAPTER 4 19
Power of Choice

CHAPTER 5 25
Building Disciples

CHAPTER 6 32
Healing the Body, Healing the Mind

Part Three
Deep Work and Self-Mastery

CHAPTER 7   40
Facing The Mirror

CHAPTER 8   46
Emotional Alchemy

CHAPTER 9   53
The Inner King Awakens

Part Four
Sharing The Light

CHAPTER 10   61
Service And Legacy

CHAPTER 11   67
Mentorship in Action

CHAPTER 12   74
Freedom Within and Without

Part Five
Tool For Life

CHAPTER 13   81
Practices for Transformation

CHAPTER 14   87
The King's Reflection

Work Cited   90

Foreword

Mentoring the Kings draws upon the transformative journeys of individuals who have risen above their past to reshape their future through the power of supportive mentorship. In this context, experience becomes the greatest teacher, and mentorship is the guiding principle.

The stories shared within these pages are narratives of resilience, soul-searching, and renewal, guided by mentors committed to fostering change and success. This book creates a sanctuary for self-discovery, encouraging readers to confront the root of their struggles—thoughts, emotions, and desires—

while practicing self-discipline to navigate challenges with grace and clarity.

Through this guide, you will learn to cultivate emotional intelligence and resilience, manage stress and trauma, and embrace life's complexities with wisdom. As you embark on this mentorship journey, you will uncover practical tools for self development and unlock the latent potential that resides within you, allowing you to face challenges and rise as a victorious king.

Preface

Mentoring the Kings was created from a desire to provide guidance to those without a mentor in their immediate lives. Many have lost strength due to a lack of mentorship, guidance, and focus—necessities for maturity, navigating societal expectations, and finding purpose.

This book is designed as a compass for those seeking direction, offering wisdom derived from real-life experiences. Its purpose is to empower readers to rediscover their inner strength, transform their trajectory, and embrace the king within themselves.

Acknowlegement

To God be the glory. By His grace, these words have been brought to life, allowing us to share this wisdom with you. Let these words be a gift to you of empowerment.

Dedication and Honors

This book is dedicated to the kings who have changed their thinking, speaking and acting to change their reality and experience their life in a more positive way. This book honors the mentors who have led the way by teaching us to believe in our dreams and our hopes, to believe in ourselves.

This book is dedicated to those who are ready for change and are open to being mentored for greatness. This book is dedicated to those who are lost and are looking to understand the image of what they have become. May you see a reflection of yourself in the words to help find the king in you and rule your life with power and authority.

Message from the authors

This book **Mentoring the Kings** would be just words without the synergy, the combined efforts of billions of moments coming together in an intentional action of empathy, kindness, and mercy shown towards others through social interaction.

We bring you these words as cheat codes to move you swiftly through low vibration frequencies of depression, despair, hopelessness, and elevate into accountability, respect, responsibility and lasting transformational change.

Our efforts would not be possible without the power of the written word. If you only read these words, one aspect of your subconscious mind receives them. By speaking the words, you increase your ability to change. There is tremendous power in the spoken word and we emphasize speaking the word over yourself. Speaking a confession of faith over yourself changes your reality and future. Your past words, thoughts and imaginations have created your current reality. Your current words, thoughts and imaginations will create your future reality. Speak words of life over yourself. The tongue has the power of life and death in it. Speaking will increase your ability to change quickly and by reading and speaking words of faith over yourself more aspects of your conscious and subconscious mind are immediately renewed and you are transformed into the new reality of what you spoke.

..."The earnest heart-felt, continued prayer of a righteous man makes tremendous power available- dynamic in it working", is written in the Bible AMP, James 5:16. This book is the manifestation of much prayer and fasting. In our lives as authors, we saw miraculous transformational change and realized that these truths can assist other to quickly manifest change. These words are a plan to follow; we have provided written and spoken directions on how to bring miraculous transformational change. We are sharing the intentional miraculous transformation cheat codes to help you with just one breath feel the change.

The power of intention can be increased through prayer and fasting. These spiritual disciplines and others practices throughout the book will help you grow quickly in a relationship with yourself and God. You will read in this book how miraculous transformation takes place. Our intention is for you to experience the relationship with your Creator God, the divine. With God, everything is possible. Without God these are just words. Volumes of words can be written to emphasize how important it is to be intentional in your thoughts about yourself. It is our intention to emphasize prayer especially prayer about yourself. In the KJV Bible, 1 Thessalonians 5:17, commands us as children of God to pray without ceasing.

Let these writings be an arsenal of word weaponry for you to regain your kingdom and authority over your life.

This is our prayer, that you release and remove anything from hindering your mind from changing into your future greater self. Our prayer is that your mind is open to these simple instructions of awareness, accountability, self-respect, and responsibility through prayer and your relationship with God to mentor your king and regain authority over your life. Cover yourself in the armor of word weaponry; you are battle ready. Let your words speak your reality of power and authority over your world. Let your words be words of victory.

Let these words come alive and bring power to your life.

Moses & Sims

Introduction

Change often begins in the unlikeliest of places. Ethan's life, once a web of poor decisions and lost control, found him at the mercy of the criminal justice system. It was within the confines of a prison cell that Ethan discovered a mentor that promised to help him reclaim his life.

This book chronicles Ethan's transformative journey with his mentor, Marcus—a figure of wisdom and compassion. Marcus shares strategies for building emotional intelligence, fostering trust, and embracing change. Together, they explore godliness, spiritual growth, and the path to redemption.

Through Ethan's story, you'll reflect on the timeless question: Are kings born, or are they made? This book reveals how mentorship, emotional intelligence, and self-discipline can transform lives, guiding men toward purpose and personal growth.

In these pages, you'll witness the profound impact of mentorship through the lens of resilience, empathy, and accountability. With Marcus's guidance, Ethan learns to confront his past, master his emotions, and rebuild his life. Their story illustrates how a mentor's belief in your potential can illuminate the path to greatness.

Mentorship is not about offering easy solutions but about fostering growth through trust and action. Let these words guide you to discover the king within, empowering you to reign over your life with wisdom and strength.

Part One
The Descent and Awakening

Life often doesn't give us a guidebook, a map to navigate the chaos we inherit or create. For some, the descent into darkness feels inevitable—a product of choices, circumstances, or both. It's in this place, at our lowest, that we begin to see things for what they are.

Chapter 1
The Fall

Ethan sat on the edge of his cot, staring at the cracked tile floor of his cell. The chill from the concrete seeped into his bones, though he hardly noticed. He had become numb to the discomfort of this place, the dull ache in his back from the thin mattress, the harsh fluorescent lights buzzing overhead, the faint smell of bleach that never quite masked the staleness of the air. It had been two months, three weeks, and five days. He didn't count on purpose—it was just that the days blended together, each one indistinguishable from the last. Meals came at the same time every day, bland and predictable. Lights out was at the same time every night. The guards made their rounds with mechanical precision, their footsteps echoing down the hallway like a metronome, counting the seconds of his stagnant life. Ethan's fingers traced the edge of a worn photo on the small shelf beside him. He hesitated, then picked it up, holding it gently as if it might disintegrate. It was a picture of his little sister, Rae. She was eight when it was taken, her grin wide and missing a front tooth. He'd been 17 then, standing beside her with his arm slung protectively around her shoulders. Back then, he'd promised her the world.

"I'm gonna make it for us, Rae," he'd said, squeezing her close. "We're getting outta here." But instead of getting out, he'd dragged her deeper into the chaos.

Ethan could still hear the yelling. His father's voice, low and menacing, punctuated by the crash of something shattering against the wall. His mom's voice rising in retaliation, only to falter. They'd been at it for hours, long enough for Ethan to know it wasn't going to end until one of them left or something broke. At 12, Ethan had already learned to slip out the back door before things got too loud. He'd head to the corner store, where the older guys hung out. At first, they ignored him—just a scrawny kid trying to act tough. But he got bolder, started running errands for them. They paid him in chips and soda at first. Later, it was cash. It felt good, having something that was his. At least until it started feeling like something that owned him instead. By the time he was 16, Ethan wasn't just running errands. He was in it—deep enough that the cops knew his name, deep enough that his mom stopped asking where he was at night. The deals got bigger, the risks higher. But Ethan didn't care. As long as he could put money on the table and keep Rae smiling, it was worth it. Until it wasn't.

The memory hit him like a punch to the gut. The sound of a gunshot, sharp and deafening, still echoed in his ears. He hadn't pulled the trigger, but he might as well have. The blood on the pavement wasn't his, but it still felt like it was. They'd said it was self-defense, that the guy came at them first. But Ethan knew the truth. He'd chosen this life, and now someone else was paying the price. The weight of it sat heavy on his chest, pressing down until he could barely breathe. He ran a hand over his face, his fingers catching on the stubble he hadn't bothered to shave. This wasn't the life he'd promised Rae. This wasn't the life he'd promised himself. But promises didn't mean much when you were locked in a six-by-eight cell, eating the same bland food every day, and staring at the same damn ceiling every night. A knock on the bars broke his thoughts. "Library time," the guard said, his tone flat. Ethan didn't move at first. He wasn't in the mood to pretend to read a book, to sit in a room full of guys who were just as stuck as he was. But the alternative was staying here, alone with his thoughts. He stood, tucking Rae's photo back on the shelf. It was the only thing in this cell that felt real. As he walked down the hall, the sound of his footsteps mingling with the guard's, Ethan tried not to think about what waited for him in the library. Another hour of nothing. Another hour of pretending like this wasn't his life now. But something about today felt different, though he couldn't say why.

Instructional Break: Reflection and Tools for Change

Reflection:

Take a moment to reflect on your own life. Think of a time when you felt stuck, trapped, or like you had no way forward. What led you to that moment?

• Was it a choice you made? A situation you were born into? Or a mix of both?

• What promises—whether to yourself or others—have you struggled to keep?

• If you could take one step toward change, what would it be?

Write these thoughts in the space provided or in a journal. Remember, being honest with yourself is the first step to creating something new.

Suggested Reading:

• **Bible Passage:** 2 Corinthians 5:17 – "Therefore, if anyone is in Christ, the new creation has come: The old has gone, the new is here!"

• **Bhagavad-Gita:** Chapter 2, Verses of 47-48 – Teachings on karma and the consequences of action.

Breath work Exercise: Grounding in the Present

When life feels overwhelming, start with your breath. Try this simple practice to calm your mind:

1. Inhale deeply through your nose for 4 counts.

2. Hold your breath gently for 4 counts.

3. Exhale slowly through your mouth for 6 counts.

Repeat this cycle 5 times, allowing your shoulders to relax with each exhale.

Chapter 2
Meeting Marcus

The library smelled of stale paper and faint cleaning chemicals, a mix that somehow managed to feel both comforting and oppressive. Ethan shuffled into the room, his shoulders slouched and his head low. His eyes scanned the familiar faces scattered at the tables—a couple of guys flipping through magazines, others pretending to read while sneaking glances at the guards near the door. Ethan didn't care about books. He came to the library because it was quieter than the yard and safer than the recreation room. It was a place where he could sit unnoticed in the back corner, stare at the pages of a random textbook, and let time crawl by without anyone bothering him. Grabbing a beat-up economics book from the shelf—its spine cracked, its pages lined with faded highlighter marks—Ethan slid into his usual seat by the far wall. He flipped to a random page, his eyes glossing over the dense paragraphs without absorbing a word. It was all meaningless. But pretending to care about something, he figured, was better than letting people see how little he cared about anything. The minutes passed in silence, broken only by the shuffle of feet or the occasional murmur of conversation near the guards. Ethan settled into his usual rhythm of staring blankly at the pages when a shadow fell across the table. "Mind if I sit here?" Ethan's eyes snapped up. The man standing in front of him wasn't anyone he recognized. Tall and broad-shouldered, his presence was calm but commanding. His salt-and-pepper hair was cropped short, and his face, though lined with age, carried a softness that contrasted with the hard lines Ethan was used to seeing in this place. In one hand, the man held a small, worn book, its edges frayed as if it had been read countless times. Ethan hesitated, unsure whether to brush the man off or ignore him altogether. "It's a free country," he muttered finally, his voice laced with sarcasm. "Or so they say." The man smiled faintly, unbothered by Ethan's tone. "Good to know," he replied, pulling out the chair across from Ethan and lowering himself into it with deliberate ease. The silence stretched between them as Ethan returned to his book, though his peripheral vision stayed fixed on the stranger's steady presence. He was reading—or pretending to. Ethan couldn't tell which. After a while, the man broke the silence. "You look like someone I used to know." Ethan snorted, keeping his eyes on the page. "Yeah? Bet they didn't end up in a place like this." The man chuckled softly, his voice low and even. "Oh, I've been here before. Different walls, same prison. Anger. Regret. Pain. Those things can trap you no matter where you are." Ethan frowned, his defenses flickering. "What are you, some kind of shrink?" The man shook his head, his smile faint but unshaken. "No. Just someone who knows what it's like to feel stuck." Ethan leaned back in his chair, crossing his arms. "So what? You're here to tell me how to fix my life? Give me some magic steps to make it all better?" The man set his book down, leaning forward slightly. "Not exactly. I'm not here to fix anything. That's your job. But I can help—if you're ready to listen." Ethan scoffed, rolling his eyes. He'd heard this kind of talk before—counselors, social workers, people who thought they could save him. They didn't last. "Yeah? And what do you know about me?" he asked, his tone sharp. The man studied Ethan for a moment, his gaze steady but not intrusive. "Enough to know you're not as lost as you think. Enough to know that, deep down, you want something different. Otherwise, you wouldn't have let me sit here." Ethan's jaw tightened, his fingers curling against the edge of the table. He wanted to argue, to tell this guy he didn't know a damn thing about him. But the words wouldn't come. The man leaned back, his tone softening. "Here's the thing, Ethan. You can't control what's happened to you. None of us can. But what you can control is what you do with it. You're holding the reins—you just don't realize it yet." Ethan frowned. "Reins? What the hell are you talking about?" "It's like riding a horse," the man explained. "The horse is your life—sometimes wild, sometimes stubborn, but it moves. And you've got the reins in your hands. You can either let the horse drag you wherever it wants, or you can take control and steer." Ethan stared at him, skeptical but intrigued. "And what if I don't know where to steer?" "Then start small," the man said. "Sometimes it's not about knowing where you're going—it's about deciding not to stay where you are." Ethan fell silent, the man's words bouncing around his head. "What's your name?" the man asked after a moment. "Ethan," he muttered reluctantly. "Nice to meet you, Ethan," the man said with a small nod. "I'm Marcus."

The guard's voice interrupted them, cutting through the quiet hum of the library. "Time's up!" Ethan blinked, startled by how quickly the hour had passed. He glanced down at the open textbook, the words still as meaningless as they'd been when he first sat down. Marcus stood, slipping his worn book under his arm. "I'll see you around, Ethan," he said, his voice calm and sure.

Before Ethan could respond, Marcus turned and walked away, leaving him alone with the dog-eared textbook and a head full of questions. That night, lying on his cot, Ethan stared at the cracked ceiling. Marcus's words replayed in his mind: "You're holding the reins." He said it like it was something anyone could do. But what did that even mean? And was it even possible? As his eyes drifted shut, one thought lingered: Maybe it's time to start asking the right questions.

Instructional Break: Opening Yourself to Mentorship

Reflection:

Mentors can come in many forms—teachers, friends, strangers, or even fictional characters in a book. They don't always look like what we expect, and often, they show up when we're ready to listen. Take a moment to reflect:

- Who in your life has shown up as a guide, intentionally or unintentionally?

- What qualities do you admire in a mentor?

- Are there areas of your life where you could benefit from guidance?

- How open are you to receiving that guidance?

Write these reflections in the space provided or in a journal. If no one comes to mind as a mentor, consider what kind of mentor you'd want to meet.

Meditation Practice: Meeting Your Inner Mentor

1. Find a quiet space where you won't be disturbed. Sit comfortably and close your eyes.

2. Take a few deep breaths, feeling your body relax with each exhale.

3. Visualize yourself sitting at a table across from someone who exudes wisdom and calm. This is your inner mentor, a reflection of the guidance you seek.

4. Imagine them asking you one question:

>   What is holding you back right now?

5. Take your time to listen. There's no rush, no judgment—just an open space for reflection.

6. When you're ready, write down the insights or feelings that came to you during the meditation.

Breath work Exercise: Opening to Guidance

Use this simple breathing technique to cultivate calm and openness before seeking guidance or reflecting on your challenges.

- Inhale deeply through your nose for 4 counts.
- Hold your breath gently for 4 counts.
- Exhale slowly through your mouth for 6 counts.

Repeat this cycle 5 times. With each exhale, imagine letting go of doubt or resistance and creating space for wisdom and clarity.

Chapter 3
Re-framing the Past

Ethan couldn't get Marcus's words out of his head: "You're holding the reins." It sounded simple, even obvious, but the more he thought about it, the more complicated it felt. How could he take control of something that seemed so far gone? His life wasn't a horse—it was more like a runaway train, and every time he tried to stop it, it just picked up speed. That night, as he lay on his cot, Ethan replayed the conversation in the library. Marcus's calm confidence stuck with him, but so did his own doubt. Taking the reins sounded good in theory, but what did it mean in practice? What if he pulled the reins and the whole thing toppled over? By the time lights-out came, Ethan wasn't any closer to an answer. But for the first time in years, he felt something other than anger or despair: curiosity.

Two days later, Ethan returned to the library. He didn't bother with the economics book this time, heading straight to the table where Marcus was already sitting. The man glanced up as Ethan approached, a knowing smile playing on his lips. "You're back," Marcus said, setting his book aside. Ethan shrugged, sliding into the seat across from him. "You talk a big game," he said, his tone light but edged with skepticism. "But what does it even mean to 'take the reins'? How do you do that?" Marcus leaned back in his chair, studying Ethan for a moment. "It starts with how you see your past," he said. "If you're carrying it like a weight, it'll drag you down. But if you can see it as something you can use—as fuel —you start to take control." Ethan frowned. "Fuel? What kind of fuel comes from screwing up your life?" Marcus smiled faintly. "The kind that teaches you what you're capable of. The kind that shows you where you've been and gives you the perspective to decide where you want to go."

Marcus's Story

Marcus paused, his gaze shifting to some distant memory. "Let me tell you a story," he said. "When I was younger, I spent years blaming everyone else for my problems—my parents, my boss, the people who hurt me. I thought if I could just fight hard enough, I'd win. But all I ever did was lose. I burned bridges, pushed people away, and ended up here, in a cell, wondering how the hell my life had gone so wrong." Ethan listened, his usual skepticism tempered by curiosity. "It wasn't until someone asked me a simple question that things started to change," Marcus continued. "They asked, 'What if this isn't happening to you? What if it's happening for you?'" Ethan's brow furrowed. "What the hell does that mean?" "It means every experience—good or bad—carries a lesson," Marcus said. "The question isn't 'Why me?' but 'What can I learn from this?' When I started asking that, I stopped feeling like a victim. I started seeing my mistakes as opportunities to grow." Ethan leaned back in his chair, his arms crossed. "That sounds like some self-help garbage." Marcus chuckled. "Maybe it is. But it worked for me. And if you're sitting here, asking questions, maybe it could work for you too."

Ethan's First Step

Later that evening Ethan lay awake in his cell, staring at the cracked ceiling. Marcus's words rattled around in his head, challenging the way he saw his own life. "What can I learn from this?" The question made him uncomfortable. His past wasn't something he wanted to learn from—it was something he wanted to forget. But Marcus had made it sound like forgetting wasn't the answer. Maybe learning was. He reached under his mattress and pulled out the small notebook he hadn't touched in weeks. Flipping to a blank page, he sat for a long time, his pen hovering over the paper.

Finally, he wrote:

- *Mom's fights taught me how to stand my ground.*
- *Running errands taught me how to hustle.*
- *Losing Rae's trust taught me what matters most.*

The words looked strange on the page, like they didn't belong to him. But the longer he stared at them, the more they started to feel like something else—something useful. For the first time, his past didn't feel like a chain holding him down. It felt like bricks. Heavy, sure, but maybe, just maybe, he could use them to build something.

Instructional Break: Re-framing the Past

Reflection Questions:

Think about your own life. What experiences have shaped you? They don't have to be positive—sometimes, the hardest moments teach us the most. Ask yourself:

- What events or decisions in my life have felt like mistakes or failures?
- What lessons can I take from those experiences?
- How can I use what I've learned to grow or help others?

Write these reflections in the space provided or in a journal. Focus on the lessons rather than the pain.

Suggested Readings and Reflection:

1. Tao Te Ching (Verse 64): Reflect on the idea of small actions leading to profound change.

2. The Alchemist by Paulo Coelho: Consider Santiago's journey and how each obstacle brought him closer to his treasure.

3. Bible Passage: Romans 8:28 – "And we know that in all things God works for the good of those who love him, who have been called according to his purpose."

4. Bhagavad-Gita: Chapter 6, Verse 5 – Teachings on self-mastery and turning challenges into opportunities.

Breath work for Reflection:

When reflecting on painful memories, emotions can rise to the surface. Use this breathing exercise to stay grounded:

1. Inhale for 4 counts, focusing on the word *learn*.

2. Hold for 4 counts, focusing on *strength*.

3. Exhale for 6 counts, releasing tension or doubt.

Repeat for 5 cycles.

Journaling Exercise:

Write down three difficult experiences from your life. For each one, ask:

• What did this experience teach me?

• How can I use this lesson in my life moving forward?

Part Two
Foundations of Change

Change is never easy. It requires not just a shift in perspective but deliberate, consistent effort to rebuild what was once broken. This isn't about quick fixes or sudden breakthroughs. Change is slow, uncomfortable, and often messy. But it starts with small choices—the kind that might seem insignificant in the moment but add up to something greater over time.

Chapter 4
Power of Choice

Ethan sat on his cot, staring at the notebook in his hands. It had been two days since he'd written that list—three simple lines that felt heavier with meaning every time he looked at them.

Mom's fights taught me how to stand my ground.

Running errands taught me how to hustle.

Losing Rae's trust taught me what matters most.

At first, the words felt foreign, like they belonged to someone else. But the more he thought about them, the more he realized Marcus might be onto something. Maybe his past wasn't just a collection of failures. Maybe it was something he could use.

But how? That question gnawed at him as he walked into the library for their next meeting. Marcus was waiting at their usual table, the same worn book in hand. He looked up as Ethan approached, a small smile breaking across his face. "You look like a man with questions," Marcus said, closing his book and gesturing for Ethan to sit. Ethan dropped into the chair, setting the notebook on the table. "You said something last time about taking the reins," he began. "And I get it—kind of. But how do you actually do that? How do you stop feeling like life is just... happening to you?" Marcus leaned back in his chair, his gaze steady. "It starts with a choice," he said. "Not a big one. Just the choice to see things differently. To stop asking, 'Why is this happening to me?' and start asking, 'What can I do with this?'" Ethan frowned. "That sounds great and all, but what does it actually look like? What do you *do* with it?"

Marcus smiled faintly. "You start small. Every choice you make—what you say, how you react, what you focus on—those are all steps. You don't have to fix everything overnight. You just have to decide which way you want to go." Marcus reached into his pocket and pulled out a small, chipped domino, placing it on the table. "You ever play dominoes?" he asked. Ethan nodded. "Yeah, back when I was a kid." Marcus tapped the domino with his finger. "When you knock one over, it doesn't just fall, right? It sets off the next one, and the next one, until the whole line moves. That's how choices work. One small action can set off a chain reaction, for better or worse." Ethan stared at the domino, his mind flickering back to moments in his own life. Skipping school that one day had led to running with the wrong crowd. Losing Rae's trust had spiraled into shutting everyone out. One choice always seemed to lead to another, but he'd never thought about it the other way around—about how one *good* choice might do the same. "So, what? I'm just supposed to start pushing over good dominoes?" he asked, his tone skeptical but not dismissive. Marcus chuckled. "Something like that. But it's not about getting it right every time. It's about being intentional. Start with one small thing. That's all it takes to shift the momentum."

Chapter 4

Marcus opened his book to a passage and slid it across the table to Ethan. The words were from the *Tao Te Ching*:

> "A journey of a thousand miles begins with a single step."

Ethan read the line twice, then looked up. "So, what's the step?"

Marcus leaned forward, his tone gentle but firm. "That's for you to decide. Maybe it's writing something down every morning. Maybe it's pausing before you react. Maybe it's as simple as choosing not to let one bad moment ruin your whole day."

Ethan thought about the notebook under his cot, the list he'd started. He could do that—write one thing every morning. It didn't seem like much, but maybe that was the point.

Marcus smiled, as if he could see Ethan's thoughts taking shape. "You don't need to know the whole path right now," he said. "Just the next step. That's all."

For the next week, Ethan tried. Each morning, he wrote down one small intention:

> Stay calm. Think before you act. Be open

It felt awkward at first, like he was pretending to be someone he wasn't. But something strange happened. On the third day, when another inmate bumped into him in the lunch line, Ethan paused before snapping back. He could feel the anger bubbling up, the words ready to fly out of his mouth—but he remembered his intention: *Stay calm*. He didn't say anything. And while it felt weird to let it go, it also felt... lighter.

At their next meeting, Marcus introduced Ethan to another teaching. He opened a copy of the Quran and read aloud:

> "Indeed, Allah will not change the condition of a people until they change what is in themselves." *(Quran 13:11)*

Ethan frowned, the words sinking in. "So it's on me," he said finally.

Marcus nodded. "Exactly. Change doesn't happen to you—it happens through you. That's the power of choice. Every small decision you make shapes who you're becoming." It wasn't easy. Some days, Ethan forgot to write in his notebook. Other days, he got so angry he couldn't stop himself from snapping at someone. But each time he fell off track, he remembered Marcus's words:

> "Discipline isn't about never failing—it's about starting again every time you do."

By the end of the week, Ethan noticed something. His choices—small as they were—were starting to add up. The days felt a little less heavy, a little more his own. For the first time, Ethan felt like he was steering, even if just a little.

∼

Chapter 4

Instructional Break: The Ripple Effect of Choices

Reflection Section:

Think about your own decisions:

- What are three recent choices you've made that moved you closer to or further from your goals?

- Are there patterns in your decision-making you'd like to change?

- What is one intentional choice you can make today to step toward the life you want?

Write these reflections in the space provided or in a journal. Focus on the decisions rather than the pain.

Suggested Reading and Reflection:

1. The Alchemist by Paulo Coelho – Reflect on how Santiago's choice to leave his sheep set him on a life-changing journey. Ask yourself: *What is my Personal Legend, and what small choice can I make to pursue it?*

2. Tao Te Ching (Verse 64): "A journey of a thousand miles begins with a single step." Reflect on how even the smallest actions build toward transformation.

3. The Quran (13:11): Consider the idea that change begins within.

4. The Story of Buddha – Consider Siddhartha Gautama's decision to leave comfort for growth. Ask: *What comfort am I clinging to that's keeping me from moving forward?*

Experiment: Small Steps, Big Changes

For the next seven days, identify one small, intentional choice you can make each day to shift your energy toward growth.

• Examples: Writing one positive thought in a journal, pausing before reacting in frustration, or prioritizing mindfulness for five minutes.

Breath work and Energy Practice:

Use this technique to align your energy with intentional choices:

1. Sit comfortably and close your eyes.

2. Inhale deeply for 4 counts, visualizing clarity entering your mind.

3. Hold your breath for 4 counts, imagining that clarity settling in your heart.

4. Exhale slowly for 6 counts, releasing doubt and resistance.

Repeat for 5 cycles, focusing on the word *choice*.

Chapter 5
Building Disciples

Ethan sat at the same library table where he'd first met Marcus, the notebook in front of him filled with scattered thoughts, phrases, and ideas. Over the past few weeks, he'd started showing up for himself in ways he hadn't before—writing in the mornings, choosing calm over chaos, even thinking twice before reacting to someone else bad energy. But today, as he stared at the blank page, he felt stuck.

The past few days had been rough. A fight in the yard had stirred up the usual anger and frustration, and despite his attempts to stay grounded, he'd lashed out at one of the guards. Now, the familiar weight of shame was settling in again.

When Marcus arrived, Ethan didn't bother hiding his frustration. "I don't get it," he said before Marcus could even sit down. "I'm trying, but it feels like one step forward, two steps back. What's the point of showing up if it doesn't stick?"

Marcus raised an eyebrow, his calm demeanor unwavering. "Let me guess—you think you're supposed to have it all figured out by now?"

Ethan shrugged. "I mean, isn't that the point? Taking the reins, making better choices... It's supposed to get easier, right?"

Marcus smiled faintly. "Ethan, discipline isn't about getting it right every time. It's about starting again every time you fall. That's how you build the muscle."

The Foundation of Discipline

Marcus leaned back in his chair, folding his hands on the table. "Think of discipline like a house," he said. "The foundation is your why—why you're doing this work, why it matters to you. Without that, everything else falls apart. So, what's your why?"

Ethan frowned, caught off guard. He hadn't thought about it that way before. "I don't know," he admitted. "Maybe... I just don't want to feel like this anymore. Like I'm stuck."

"That's a start," Marcus said, nodding. "Now build on it. What's one thing you can do every day to remind yourself of that why? Something small. Something doable."

Ethan thought for a moment. "I guess... writing helps. Even if it feels stupid sometimes, it's like... I'm checking in with myself."

"Good," Marcus said. "That's your anchor. Now let's talk about structure."

Creating a Routine

Marcus pulled out his notebook and flipped to a page filled with short lists and scribbled notes. "A routine isn't about boxing yourself in," he explained. "It's about giving yourself a framework—a way to create stability when everything else feels unstable."

He slid the notebook across the table, pointing to a simple list:

- Morning: Write one intention for the day.

- Afternoon: Take five deep breaths before reacting to anything stressful.

- Evening: Reflect on one thing you did well, no matter how small.

"This isn't about perfection," Marcus said. "It's about consistency. Even if you miss a day, the routine is still there, waiting for you. The act of coming back to it—that's where the growth happens."

Ethan nodded, his mind already running through how he could adapt this to his own day. "Okay, but what about when it feels impossible? Like when you're too mad or too tired to even try?"

Marcus leaned forward, his gaze steady. "That's when discipline matters most. Showing up when it's hard—that's how you prove to yourself that you can. Even if all you do is write one word or take one breath, you've still shown up. And that's enough."

The Archer's Lesson

Marcus opened another book, this one thinner and more delicate. "This is from the *Tao Te Ching*," he said, flipping to a marked page.

Ethan leaned in as Marcus read aloud:

"A skilled archer doesn't wait for the perfect conditions to practice. They refine their aim every day, so when the moment comes, they are ready."

Marcus closed the book, meeting Ethan's eyes. "The archer doesn't practice because it's easy or convenient. They practice because they know that every small step prepares them for the bigger ones. That's what you're doing here—refining your aim, one day at a time."

Ethan's Breakthrough

Over the next week, Ethan worked on building his routine. He started small, sticking to one thing: writing an intention in his notebook each morning. Some days, it was a single word:

> Try. Calm. Breathe.

Other days, he wrote out his frustrations, using the page as a place to unload the anger and doubt that threatened to derail him.

At first, it felt awkward. But by the third day, he noticed a difference. The act of writing gave him a moment to pause, to center himself before the chaos of the day began.

Chapter 5

One afternoon, an argument broke out in the lunch line. Ethan felt the familiar surge of anger rising, his body tensing as the urge to lash out crept in. But then he remembered what he'd written that morning:

> Pause before you react.

He took a deep breath. And then another. The tension eased, and instead of snapping, he stepped back and let it go.

For the first time, Ethan felt like he was steering—not perfectly, but enough to make a difference.

Instructional Break: Building Your Discipline Muscle

Reflection Questions:

• What is one area of your life where you struggle with consistency?

• How do you currently view discipline—as a punishment or as a tool for growth?

• What is one small, actionable habit you can start today to strengthen your discipline muscle?

Write these reflections in the space provided or in a journal. Focus on discipline rather than the pain.

Practice: Building a Routine for Growth

1. Identify one habit to focus on (e.g., journaling, mindful breathing, or stretching).

2. Commit to it for at least five minutes each day for one week.

3. Track your progress and reflect on how it feels to show up consistently.

Breath work for Focus and Persistence:

1. Sit comfortably with your eyes closed.

2. Inhale deeply for 4 counts, focusing on the word *focus*.

3. Hold your breath for 4 counts, imagining steadiness settling in your heart.

4. Exhale slowly for 6 counts, releasing frustration or doubt.

Repeat for 5 cycles.

Chapter 6
Healing the Body, Healing the Mind

Ethan leaned back against the wall of the library, the notebook resting on his knee. Over the past few weeks, his routine had become a small but steady part of his day. Writing down intentions each morning, pausing before reacting, and reflecting in the evenings had helped him feel a little more in control. But something still gnawed at him—a tension he couldn't shake, no matter how many deep breaths he took or words he wrote.

When Marcus walked in, Ethan didn't wait for the usual small talk. "What do you do with the stuff you can't control?" he asked. "The anger that just sits there, the stress that doesn't go away no matter what you do?"

Marcus set his book down and pulled out the chair across from him. "That's a good question," he said, his voice calm. "Most of us walk around carrying things we don't even realize—stress, anger, guilt—and it builds up in our bodies. If you don't release it, it just... stays there."

Ethan frowned, leaning forward. "What, like... energy?"

"Exactly," Marcus said. "Your body and mind are connected. You can't heal one without healing the other. That's why we're going to talk about how to take care of both."

The Mind-Body Connection

Marcus began by explaining the connection between physical health and emotional well-being.

"Think about it," he said. "When you're stressed, your shoulders tense up. When you're angry, your jaw tightens. Your emotions don't just live in your head—they live in your body too."

Ethan nodded, thinking about the times he'd felt his chest tighten with frustration or his stomach churn with anxiety. "So, what do you do about it?" he asked.

"You move," Marcus replied simply. "You breathe. You listen to your body and give it what it needs. Sometimes that means eating better. Sometimes it means stretching, walking, or just sitting still and letting yourself feel."

Small Steps to Healing

Marcus pulled out a scrap of paper and wrote down a short list:

1. Start with your breath:

• "Your breath is the quickest way to calm your mind and body," Marcus said. "When you're stressed, try this: inhale deeply for 4 counts, hold for 4 counts, and exhale for 6. Do that five times and see how you feel."

2. Move your body:

• "It doesn't have to be complicated," Marcus explained. "Try stretching your arms overhead, rolling your shoulders, or even standing up and sitting back down a few times. Movement releases tension."

3. Pay attention to what you eat:

• "Food isn't just fuel—it's medicine," Marcus said. "When you can, choose things that make your body feel good. Drink water. Eat whole foods when you get the chance. It doesn't have to be perfect, just better."

4. Rest:

• "Your body can't heal if you never give it a break," Marcus added. "That doesn't just mean sleep—it means finding moments of stillness throughout your day."

Chapter 6

Ethan glanced at the list, feeling a mix of curiosity and doubt. "This seems... simple," he said.

"It is," Marcus replied. "But simple doesn't mean easy. The hard part is sticking with it. That's where discipline comes in."

Healing Through Movement

The next time they met, Marcus introduced Ethan to a few simple movements he could do in his cell.

"Try this," Marcus said, standing and demonstrating. "Plant your feet firmly on the ground, about hip-width apart. Bend your knees slightly so they are not locked, tilt your pelvis slightly forward, feel as if there is a cord coming from the top of your head pulling your spine straight, square your shoulders, open your hands palms facing forward Lift your arms overhead, reaching toward the ceiling. This is called Mountain Pose—it's a yoga posture that builds strength and focus."

Ethan stood and mimicked the pose, feeling the stretch in his legs and back.

"Hold it for a few breaths," Marcus said. "Notice how your body feels. Strong, steady, grounded."

When Ethan sat back down, he felt a strange sense of calm—not the kind that came from being still, but from moving with intention.

Lessons from Other Traditions

As they wrapped up, Marcus shared a story from the *Bhagavad-Gita*, an ancient Indian text.

"It's about a warrior named Arjuna," Marcus said. "He's about to go into battle, but he's paralyzed by doubt and fear. His guide, Krishna, teaches him that the body and mind must work together. You can't fight a battle if your body is weak or your mind is scattered. Both need to be in balance."

Ethan leaned back, letting the words sink in. "So, this is like my battle," he said finally. "Not just the one in my head, but the one in my body too."

Marcus smiled. "Exactly. And every small step you take—every stretch, every breath, every better choice you make—is a step toward winning that battle."

Chapter 6

Instructional Break: Healing the Body, Healing the Mind

Reflection Questions:

• How does stress show up in your body? Tight shoulders? A clenched jaw?

• What's one small thing you can do today to care for your body—stretching, breathing, or drinking water?

• How might taking care of your body help ease your mind?

Write these reflections in the space provided or in a journal. Focus on the body rather than the pain.

Suggested Readings and Reflection:

1 Bhagavad-Gita: Reflect on the balance between action and stillness in Arjuna's journey.

2 Tao Te Ching (Verse 10): Consider the harmony of body, mind, and spirit.

3 The Alchemist: Reflect on how physical and spiritual alignment helped Santiago stay on his path.

Practice: Small Steps to Healing

Breathing Exercise:

- Sit comfortably with your feet flat on the ground.
- Inhale deeply for 4 counts, hold for 4 counts, and exhale slowly for 6.
- Repeat 5 times, focusing on releasing tension with each breath.

Movement Exercise:

- Try the Warrior Pose:
- Stand with your feet hip-width apart.
- Bend your knees slightly and lift your arms overhead.
- Hold for 3–5 breaths, feeling the strength in your legs and the stretch in your arms.

Nutrition Exercise:

- Drink a glass of water with intention, thinking about how it nourishes your body.

Part Three
Deep Work and Self-Mastery

Transformation begins when we're willing to go beyond the surface. The first steps—acknowledging the need for change, building new habits, and creating structure—are necessary, but they are only the beginning. Deep work is not for the faint of heart. It means confronting the hardest truths about ourselves, facing the emotions we've buried, and challenging the narratives we've used to define who we are. It's uncomfortable, messy, and often painful. But it's also where the magic happens.

Chapter 7
Facing the Mirror

The mornings had become a quiet ritual for Ethan. He would wake, sit on the edge of his cot, and open his notebook. Some days he wrote intentions; other days, he scribbled fragments of thoughts he didn't fully understand. The routine steadied him, but it also brought something unexpected: a sense of unease.

As Ethan wrote, he couldn't help but notice the weight of his own words. The anger, the regrets, the excuses—they stared back at him like accusations. He felt as if the pages were holding up a mirror, forcing him to confront the parts of himself he'd spent years trying to ignore.

That afternoon, in the library, he told Marcus about it.

"It's like I'm seeing myself for the first time," Ethan said, his voice low. "And I don't like what I see."

Marcus nodded, his expression thoughtful. "That's the hard part," he said. "Most people spend their whole lives running from their reflection. But if you want to change, you have to face it.

You have to own every part of it—the good, the bad, and the ugly."

Marcus leaned forward, his tone firm but kind. "Ethan, if you're going to rebuild, you have to start with the truth. Not the version of yourself you show other people, but the one you hide—even from yourself."

Ethan frowned, crossing his arms. "And what if I don't like what I find?"

"Then you have a choice," Marcus said. "You can keep running from it, or you can use it. The truth isn't there to tear you down—it's there to set you free."

He reached into his pocket and pulled out a folded piece of paper. Unfolding it, he slid it across the table to Ethan.

"What's this?" Ethan asked, picking it up.

"A question," Marcus said. "One that changed everything for me."

Ethan read the words aloud: *What am I pretending not to know?*

The question hit like a punch to the gut. Ethan stared at the paper, his mind racing.

Marcus's voice softened. "Answering that question is hard—painful, even. But it's where the real work begins. Because once you stop pretending, you can start changing."

That night, Ethan sat on his cot with the piece of paper in one hand and his notebook in the other. He stared at the question for what felt like hours.

What am I pretending not to know?

Chapter 7

The answer came slowly, haltingly, but when it did, it spilled out in a rush:

- *That I'm angry because I'm scared.*
- *That I pushed Rae away because I didn't think I deserved her.*
- *That I let myself end up here because it was easier than fighting to be better.*

The words felt raw, like an open wound. But as painful as they were, they also felt... honest. For the first time, Ethan wasn't hiding.

When Ethan met Marcus again, he handed him the notebook without a word. Marcus flipped through the pages, nodding as he read.

"This is good," Marcus said finally. "Hard, but good. The truth is where healing starts."

He closed the notebook and looked at Ethan. "Now, let's take it a step further. I want you to look in the mirror—literally. Stand in front of it, look yourself in the eyes, and say, 'I see you. I accept you.'"

Ethan recoiled. "That sounds... weird."

"It is," Marcus admitted with a small smile. "But it's also powerful. You've spent years looking away from yourself, avoiding what's there. This is about seeing yourself fully—flaws and all—and accepting that you're still worthy of healing.

To help Ethan understand the importance of self-honesty, Marcus shared a story from *The Alchemist*.

"Santiago, the shepherd, spends his whole journey searching for treasure," Marcus said. "But in the end, he realizes the treasure was inside him all along. He just had to face himself to find it."

Ethan nodded, the metaphor sinking in. "So, this is my treasure hunt," he said. "But instead of gold, it's... me."

Marcus smiled. "Exactly. And the more honest you are with yourself, the closer you get to finding it."

Ethan's Small Victory

Later that evening Ethan stood in front of the small mirror in his cell. His reflection stared back at him, tired and wary. For a long moment, he couldn't say anything.

But then, in a voice barely above a whisper, he said, "I see you."

His reflection didn't change, but something inside him did. The words felt awkward, uncomfortable—but also true.

Ethan exhaled, his shoulders relaxing. He wasn't where he wanted to be, but for the first time, he felt like he was moving in the right direction.

Instructional Break: Facing the Mirror

Reflection Questions:

• What truths about yourself have you been avoiding?

• How might acknowledging those truths help you move forward?

• What's one small step you can take today to face your reflection?

Write these reflections in the space provided or in a journal. Focus on the yourself rather than the pain.

Suggested Readings and Reflection:

1. *The Alchemist* by Paulo Coelho: Reflect on Santiago's journey to self-discovery.

2. *Bhagavad-Gita*: Consider Arjuna's moment of self-confrontation before stepping into his purpose.

3. *Tao Te Ching* (Verse 33): Reflect on the line,

> "Knowing others is intelligence; knowing yourself is true wisdom."

Practice: The Reflection Exercise

1. Stand in front of a mirror, alone and undistracted.

2. Look yourself in the eyes and say aloud: "I see you. I accept you."

3. Notice any emotions that come up. Write them down in a journal or notebook afterward.

Breath work for Self-Acceptance:

1. Inhale deeply for 4 counts, focusing on the word *accept*.

2. Hold for 4 counts, imagining self-compassion filling your heart.

3. Exhale slowly for 6 counts, releasing judgment or doubt.

Repeat for 5 cycles.

Chapter 8
Emotional Alchemy

Ethan sat at the library table, his notebook open to the words he'd written that morning: I see you. I accept you. I'm ready to try.

He traced the edges of the letters with his finger, feeling a strange mixture of pride and discomfort. Accepting himself—even just saying the words—had been harder than he'd expected. But something about it had also felt... freeing.

When Marcus arrived, he slid into the chair across from Ethan and glanced at the notebook. "Still showing up," Marcus said with a small nod of approval.

Ethan smirked. "Barely."

Marcus chuckled, but his expression turned serious. "Accepting yourself is a big step," he said. "But it's not the only one. You've seen the truth about where you are. Now it's time to decide what to do with it."

Ethan frowned, leaning back in his chair. "What do you mean?"

"I mean turning the weight you're carrying into fuel," Marcus said. "Emotions—anger, fear, shame—they're powerful. But they don't have to control you. You can use them."

The Fire Inside

Ethan's frown deepened. "Use them? How? It's not like I can just decide not to be pissed off or scared."

"No, you can't," Marcus said. "But you can decide what to do with it. Think of your emotions like fire. It can burn you, or it can keep you warm. It all depends on how you use it."

Ethan stared at him, skeptical. "And how am I supposed to do that?"

Marcus pulled out his worn book and flipped to a page marked with a folded corner. "Let me tell you a story," he said. "It's about a man who learned how to turn his anger into compassion."

The story was from the *Bhagavad-Gita*, about a warrior named Arjuna. Torn between his duty and his fear, Arjuna was paralyzed, unable to act. His guide, Krishna, taught him that his emotions weren't the enemy—they were a tool. By channeling his fear into focus and his anger into determination, Arjuna was able to find clarity and step into his purpose.

Ethan listened quietly, the words sinking in. "So, you're saying I'm supposed to turn my anger into... what? Motivation?"

"Something like that," Marcus said. "But it starts with understanding your emotions—where they come from, what they're trying to tell you. Only then can you transform them."

Facing the Storm

That night, back in his cell, Ethan sat with his notebook, the question from earlier still echoing in his mind: *What is my anger trying to tell me?*

The answer didn't come right away. He sat there for what felt like hours, his pen hovering over the page. Finally, he started to write:

- *I'm angry because I feel trapped.*
- *I'm angry because I'm scared I'll never get out of here.*
- *I'm angry because I think it's too late to change.*

The words felt raw, almost too painful to look at. But as they filled the page, Ethan felt the fire inside him begin to shift. His anger wasn't just anger—it was fear, regret, and a longing for something better.

And for the first time, he wondered if maybe that fire could be used for something else.

The Practice of Emotional Alchemy

The next time Ethan met Marcus, he told him about what he'd written. Marcus listened carefully, then nodded. "Good," he said. "You're starting to see what's underneath the anger. That's the first step."

"What's the next one?" Ethan asked.

Marcus smiled. "Turning it into something useful."

He leaned forward, his voice steady. "When you feel anger, don't push it away. Sit with it. Breathe through it. Ask yourself what it's trying to tell you. Then decide how you want to use that energy. Maybe it's to stand up for yourself. Maybe it's to push through something hard. Whatever it is, let it fuel you, not control you."

Small Steps Toward Transformation

Over the next week, Ethan practiced what Marcus had taught him. Whenever he felt anger bubbling up, he stopped, took a deep breath, and asked himself: *What is this trying to tell me?*

Sometimes the answers surprised him. Other times, they didn't come at all. But even the act of pausing felt like progress.

One afternoon, when another inmate shoved him in the yard, Ethan felt the familiar surge of rage. His fists clenched, his breath quickened, and for a moment, he was ready to fight.

But then Marcus's words came back to him: *Let it fuel you, not control you.*

Ethan stepped back, took a deep breath, and walked away. The fire didn't disappear, but it didn't burn him, either.

Chapter 8

That night, he wrote in his notebook:

> I didn't fight today. I chose something better.

It wasn't perfect. But it was progress.

Instructional Break: Emotional Alchemy

Reflection Questions:

• What emotions feel the hardest for you to manage?

• What do you think those emotions might be trying to tell you?

• How can you use those emotions as fuel for growth instead of letting them control you?

Write these reflections in the space provided or in a journal. Focus on the emotions rather than the pain.

Practice: Turning Emotions into Fuel

• **Pause:** When you feel a strong emotion, stop and take three deep breaths.

• **Reflect:** Ask yourself, "What is this trying to tell me?"

• **Act:** Decide how you want to use that emotion. Write down one small action you can take.

Breath work for Emotional Release:

• Inhale deeply for 4 counts, focusing on the word *release*.

• Hold your breath for 4 counts, imagining the emotion settling into clarity.

• Exhale slowly for 6 counts, letting go of tension or frustration.

Repeat for 5 cycles.

Suggested Readings:

1. *Bhagavad-Gita*: Reflect on Arjuna's journey of transforming fear into purpose.

2. *The Tao Te Ching* (Verse 26): Consider the balance between stillness and action.

3. *The Alchemist* by Paulo Coelho: Reflect on the power of using obstacles as stepping stones.

Chapter 9
The Inner King Awakens

Ethan stood at the edge of the yard, his hands shoved deep into his pockets as the cool morning air pressed against his skin. The notebook, now well-worn and filled with months of scribbled thoughts, rested against his chest under his folded arms. For the first time, he felt like the words inside weren't just a reflection of who he was—they were a map for who he could become.

The anger that had once defined him had shifted into something else. It still burned, but now it felt less like a wildfire and more like a controlled flame—a source of heat, light, and power.

That afternoon, he met Marcus in the library. Ethan dropped into his usual chair, his notebook resting on the table.

"I've been thinking about something," Ethan said.

Marcus raised an eyebrow, closing the book in his hands. "What's on your mind?"

Ethan leaned forward, his elbows on the table. "What you said before, about turning emotions into fuel—it's been helping. But I keep thinking... If I can do that, what else am I capable of?"

Marcus smiled faintly, leaning back in his chair. "That's the right question, Ethan. And the answer? A lot more than you think."

Recognizing the Inner King

Marcus tapped the table lightly with his fingers. "Let me ask you something. When you picture yourself—not the version of you sitting here now, but the version you want to be—what do you see?"

Ethan frowned, his brow furrowing. "I don't know. I guess... someone who's got it together. Someone who doesn't let things get to him. Someone who's... in charge of his life."

Marcus nodded. "That's a good start. But let's take it further. What does that version of you believe about himself? How does he carry himself? How does he treat the people around him?"

Ethan hesitated, the questions catching him off guard. "I guess... he's confident. Respectful. Not just to other people, but to himself."

"That's the inner king," Marcus said simply. "The part of you that's always been there, waiting for you to step into it."

Ethan snorted, leaning back in his chair. "A king? In here? I don't think so."

Marcus smiled faintly. "A king isn't defined by where he is, Ethan. He's defined by how he chooses to show up—no matter where he's standing."

. . .

Stepping into Power

For the next week, Marcus challenged Ethan to act as if he were already the man he wanted to become. "Every choice you make," Marcus had said, "is a step toward or away from that version of yourself. So start choosing like the king you are."

At first, it felt awkward—almost like pretending. But slowly, Ethan started to notice small changes. He held his head higher when he walked through the yard. He chose his words more carefully when talking to the other inmates. And when tension flared, he reminded himself that power didn't mean lashing out—it meant staying steady.

One morning, as Ethan scribbled in his notebook, a thought struck him:

> What if being a king isn't about controlling others? What if it's about mastering myself?

The idea settled deep in his chest, both foreign and familiar.

The Lion's Heart

During one of their meetings, Marcus introduced Ethan to a visualization exercise.

"Close your eyes," Marcus instructed. "I want you to picture a lion."

Ethan closed his eyes, the image of the great animal forming in his mind.

"Think about what makes the lion powerful," Marcus continued. "It's not just his strength. It's his presence. He doesn't need to prove himself. He just is. That's the kind of power I'm talking about—the kind that comes from within."

As Ethan breathed deeply, the image of the lion grew sharper. He imagined the steadiness in the lion's gaze, the quiet strength in the way it moved.

When Ethan opened his eyes, Marcus was watching him closely. "That's the king inside you," Marcus said. "The one who knows his worth, no matter what anyone else says."

A Test of Strength

A few days later, Ethan found himself in the middle of a tense situation in the yard. An argument had broken out between two inmates, and the energy was escalating quickly.

The old Ethan would have jumped in, either to break it up or to escalate it further. But now, he paused. He thought about the lion, the steady strength it carried. Instead of reacting, Ethan stepped back and watched.

When one of the inmates turned to him, clearly expecting him to take sides, Ethan shook his head. "Not today," he said simply.

The tension fizzled, and the other inmate turned away. Ethan exhaled slowly, feeling a quiet pride settle in his chest.

The Awakening

That night, as he sat on his cot, Ethan flipped back through his notebook. The pages were filled with reflections, intentions, and small victories. For the first time, he could see the threads of a new version of himself taking shape.

He wrote at the top of a blank page:

> I am not the man I was. I am the man I am becoming.

And for the first time, he believed it.

Instructional Break: Awakening the Inner King

Reflection Questions:

- How do you define personal power?

- What version of yourself do you want to become?

- What choices can you make today that align with that version of yourself?

Write these reflections in the space provided or in a journal. Focus on the yourself rather than the pain.

Practice: Visualization for Confidence

1. Close your eyes and picture a lion.

2. Focus on its steady gaze, calm movements, and undeniable presence.

3. Imagine embodying that same strength and confidence in your own life.

Breath work for Inner Strength:

1. Inhale deeply for 4 counts, focusing on the word *strength*.

2. Hold for 4 counts, imagining steadiness filling your chest.

3. Exhale slowly for 6 counts, releasing self-doubt.

Repeat for 5 cycles.

Suggested Readings:

1. The Bhagavad-Gita: Reflect on Arjuna stepping into his role with courage and purpose.

2. Tao Te Ching (Verse 28): Consider the balance of strength and humility.

3. The Alchemist: Reflect on Santiago's transformation as he steps into his destiny.

Part Four
Sharing The Light

Transformation isn't complete until it extends outward. Sharing the light doesn't require perfection. It requires courage—the courage to show up, to lead with empathy, and to offer what you've learned, even when you feel you're still a work in progress.

Chapter 10
Service And Legacy

Ethan sat at the library table, his hands resting on the notebook that had become his constant companion. The journey over the past few months had been intense—raw, transformative, and more difficult than he'd ever imagined. For the first time in his life, Ethan felt a flicker of pride in himself, not for what he'd done, but for who he was becoming.

But there was one question he couldn't shake: *What's next?*

Marcus joined him at the table, his usual calm energy settling over the room. Ethan wasted no time.

"So," Ethan began, "I've been doing the work. Facing myself. Making better choices. But... what happens after this? After I leave this place?"

Marcus smiled faintly. "That's a question only you can answer," he said. "But let me ask you something: What do you want to leave behind?"

Ethan frowned. "What do you mean?"

"I mean your legacy," Marcus said. "The impact you'll have on the people around you. What do you want them to remember about you? What do you want them to learn from you?"

The Ripple Effect

The idea of leaving something behind felt strange to Ethan. He'd spent so much of his life feeling like he had nothing to offer, no value to give. "How am I supposed to help anyone else," he asked, "when I'm still figuring myself out?"

Marcus leaned forward, his tone steady but insistent. "Ethan, the work you've done—facing your truth, building discipline, stepping into your power—that's not just for you. It's for everyone you meet. When you heal yourself, you create a ripple effect. Your growth inspires others to grow. Your choices show others what's possible."

Ethan nodded slowly, the weight of Marcus's words sinking in. "So, you're saying... I can be someone's Marcus?"

Marcus smiled. "Exactly. But you don't have to have all the answers to start. You just have to show up, the way someone once showed up for you."

Service in Action

Over the next few weeks, Ethan began to notice the subtle ways his growth was impacting the people around him. When tension flared in the yard, he was often the one to de-escalate it, his calm energy diffusing the situation.

One evening, a younger inmate named Jamal approached him in the rec room. "Hey," Jamal said hesitantly, "I heard you've been meeting with Marcus. He... helped you figure stuff out?"

Ethan shrugged, unsure how to respond. "Something like that," he said finally.

Jamal shifted awkwardly, glancing at the floor. "I've been feeling like... I don't know, like I'm drowning. You think he could help me too?"

Ethan studied Jamal for a moment, then nodded. "Yeah," he said. "But it starts with you. You've got to be willing to look at yourself, to do the work. It's not easy, but... it's worth it."

As Jamal walked away, Ethan felt a strange sense of responsibility settle in his chest. For the first time, he realized that his journey wasn't just about him—it was about what he could give to others.

Lessons from the Bible

During one of their meetings, Marcus shared a passage from the Bible:

> "Let your light so shine before men, that they may see your good works and glorify your Father in heaven." *(Matthew 5:16)*

Ethan frowned, the words striking a chord he hadn't expected. "So, it's not just about shining for yourself," he said slowly. "It's about helping others find their own light."

Marcus nodded. "Exactly. Service isn't about being perfect or having all the answers. It's about being a beacon—showing others what's possible by living your truth."

Ethan's Legacy

That night, Ethan sat on his cot, reflecting on the idea of legacy. For so long, he'd seen himself as a product of his mistakes, a collection of bad choices and missed opportunities. But now, he was starting to see something else: potential.

He opened his notebook and wrote:

> My legacy is not my past. My legacy is how I choose to show up today

For the first time, the thought didn't feel impossible. It felt real.

CHAPTER 10

Instructional Break: Service and Legacy

Reflection Questions:

• What impact do you want to leave on the people around you?

• How can your growth inspire others to grow?

• What small acts of service can you start today to create a positive ripple effect?

Write these reflections in the space provided or in a journal. Focus on the lessons rather than the pain.

Practice: Living Your Legacy

• **Reflect:** Write down three ways you've grown over the past month.

• **Connect:** Think of one person who might benefit from your experience.

• **Act:** Reach out to them, share your story, or offer support.

Breath work for Gratitude and Service:

1. Inhale deeply for 4 counts, focusing on the word *serve*.

2. Hold for 4 counts, imagining your light expanding outward.

3. Exhale slowly for 6 counts, releasing self-doubt.

Repeat for 5 cycles.

Suggested Readings:

1. Matthew 5:16 (Bible): Reflect on the importance of letting your light shine.

2. The Tao Te Chung (Verse 27): Consider the idea of leaving a path for others to follow.

3. Bravado-Gita: Reflect on the concept of selfless service (karma yoga).

Chapter 11
Mentorship in Action

Ethan leaned against the wall of the library, his arms crossed as he watched Jamal and Marcus talk. It had been a few weeks since Jamal had first approached him, and now the younger inmate was meeting with Marcus regularly. Then felt a quiet sense of pride watching their conversations, though he would never admit it out loud.

For the first time in his life, Then felt like he had something to offer—something real. It wasn't just about doing the work for himself anymore. He could see how his growth was beginning to ripple outward, touching the lives of others.

Later that afternoon, Marcus pulled a chair up to Then's usual table.

"So," Marcus began, his voice light but direct, "how does it feel to be a mentor?"

Then blinked, caught off guard. "Me? A mentor? I'm just telling people what you told me."

Marcus smiled faintly. "That's what mentorship is, Then. It's not about having all the answers. It's about sharing what you've learned and walking alongside someone as they find their own way."

Then shook his head, skeptical. "I don't know, man. I'm still figuring things out myself."

"Exactly," Marcus said. "You're still in it. And that's what makes you relatable. People don't need perfection—they need someone who understands where they're at because they've been there too."

Stepping Into the Role

Over the next few weeks, Ethan began to notice small changes in the way others approached him. Inmates who once barely acknowledged him started asking for advice—sometimes about Marcus, sometimes about the things he was learning.

At first, it felt strange. Ethan wasn't used to people looking up to him or valuing his perspective. But as he leaned into the role, he began to see the power in it.

One afternoon, Jamal found him sitting in the yard, his notebook balanced on his knee.

"Hey," Jamal said, sitting down beside him. "I've been thinking about what you said—that I've got to start with myself. But it's hard, man. How do you even know where to begin?"

Ethan paused, thinking back to his first conversations with Marcus. "You start small," he said finally. "Pick one thing. Like... writing down your thoughts, or taking a deep breath before you react to something. It's not about changing everything overnight—it's about showing up, one step at a time."

Jamal nodded slowly, his gaze thoughtful. "Yeah... I think I can do that."

As Jamal walked away, Ethan felt a quiet sense of fulfillment settle over him. For the first time, he understood what Marcus had meant about the ripple effect.

Lessons on Empathy

During one of their library meetings, Marcus handed Ethan a slim book. "This is something that helped me a lot when I was figuring out how to mentor others," Marcus said.

Ethan flipped through the pages, skimming the highlighted passages. It was a collection of teachings on empathy—how to listen without judgment, how to hold space for someone without trying to fix them.

Marcus leaned forward, his voice steady. "The most important thing you can give someone isn't advice—it's your attention. When you listen to someone, really listen, you're telling them they matter. And sometimes, that's enough to change everything."

Ethan nodded, the words settling deep in his chest. He thought about all the times he'd felt invisible, like no one cared enough to really hear him. The idea that he could offer someone else what he'd once needed felt... powerful.

A Test of Leadership

One day in the yard, tensions flared between two inmates over a card game. Voices rose, and Ethan could feel the energy shifting—anger bubbling to the surface, ready to boil over.

He hesitated, the old part of him itching to stay out of it, to let things play out. But then he thought of Marcus's words: *"Leadership isn't about control—it's about presence."*

Ethan stepped forward, his voice calm but firm. "Hey," he said, addressing the two men. "What's going on here?"

They turned to him, their postures tense. "This ain't got nothing to do with you, man," one of them snapped.

"Maybe not," Ethan said, holding his ground. "But I've been where you are. And I know it's not worth it. Whatever this is, it's not worth losing the progress you've made."

For a moment, the tension hung in the air. Then, slowly, the two men stepped back.

As they walked away, Ethan exhaled, his heart pounding. He wasn't sure if he'd done the right thing, but for the first time, he'd chosen to step up instead of stepping away.

Building a Legacy Together

That evening, as Ethan sat with Marcus in the library, he shared what had happened in the yard.

"You showed leadership today," Marcus said.

Ethan shrugged. "I just didn't want anyone getting hurt."

Marcus smiled. "And that's what makes you a leader. You saw a situation where you could make a difference, and you acted. That's what this is all about—using what you've learned to help others."

Ethan nodded, a small spark of pride flickering in his chest. For the first time, he could see how everything he'd been through—every mistake, every hard-earned lesson—could become something more than just his story.

It could become his legacy.

Instructional Break: Mentorship in Action

Reflection Questions:

• What lessons have you learned that you could share with someone else?

• How can you practice listening without judgment in your relationships?

• What opportunities do you have to lead by example, even in small ways?

Write these reflections in the space provided or in a journal. Focus on the relationships rather than the pain.

Practice: Active Listening

• **Be Present:** When someone speaks to you, focus entirely on them—no distractions, no interruptions.

• **Reflect Back:** Repeat what you heard to make sure you understand.

• **Hold Space:** Resist the urge to offer advice unless asked. Sometimes, just listening is enough.

Breath work for Leadership and Calm:

1. Inhale deeply for 4 counts, focusing on the word *steady*.

2. Hold for 4 counts, imagining a calm strength filling your chest.

3. Exhale slowly for 6 counts, releasing tension or doubt.

Repeat for 5 cycles.

Suggested Readings:

1. Proverbs 27:17 (Bible): "As iron sharpens iron, so one person sharpens another." Reflect on the role of mentorship in growth.

2. The Tao Te Ching (Verse 17): Consider the idea of quiet, supportive leadership.

3. The Alchemist: Reflect on how Santiago's mentors guided him toward his destiny.

Chapter 12
Freedom Within and Without

The final week of Ethan's sentence was marked by a strange mix of anticipation and unease. He'd spent so much time looking forward to the moment he could leave, imagining what life on the outside might feel like, but now that it was here, it felt... heavy.

He sat on his cot, staring at the duffel bag holding the few belongings he'd collected over the years: his notebook, a dog-eared paperback Marcus had lent him, and a stack of letters from his sister, Rae.

Marcus had always told him,

> "Freedom doesn't start when you walk out of here. It starts when you decide to take control of your life."

Ethan wanted to believe that was true. He'd done the work—faced his past, built new habits, and begun to see himself in a new light. But the fear still lingered. What if the outside world was too much? What if he slipped back into old patterns?

The next day, Marcus found him sitting alone in the yard.

"You ready?" Marcus asked, lowering himself onto the bench beside him.

Ethan shrugged, his gaze fixed on the horizon. "I don't know. I've been waiting for this day for so long, but now that it's here..."

"You're scared," Marcus finished for him.

Ethan nodded. "Yeah."

Marcus leaned forward, resting his elbows on his knees. "That fear is normal. But it's not a reason to stop. You've built something solid, Ethan. Something no one can take from you. The man you've become in here—the one who's learned to face himself, to choose better, to lead with strength—that man is real. He's you."

Ethan exhaled, the tension in his chest easing just a little.

The Final Lesson

That evening, in their last library session, Marcus handed Ethan a folded piece of paper. "Take this with you," he said.

Ethan unfolded it to find a list of three questions:

1 What kind of man do I want to be today?

2 What choices align with that vision?

3 What can I do to serve others and myself?

Ethan stared at the words, his throat tightening. "You really think I'm ready for this?"

Marcus smiled faintly. "I know you are. The only question is whether you believe it."

Stepping Through the Gate

The morning of his release was quiet. Ethan stood in the intake room, signing the last of the paperwork that would officially set him free. The guard handed him the bag with his belongings and pointed him toward the exit.

As Ethan stepped through the gates, the sunlight hit him like a wave—warm, bright, and almost overwhelming. He paused, letting the moment sink in.

The world felt bigger than he remembered, and for the first time, it didn't scare him.

A Ritual for New Beginnings

Later that day, Ethan found a quiet spot in a nearby park. He sat under a tree, his notebook open on his lap, and wrote:

> This is the beginning. Not just of my freedom,
> but of my life. The man I was, brought me
> here. The man I am will take me forward.
> And the man I'm becoming will light the way
> for others.

He closed the notebook and took a deep breath, letting the air fill his lungs. For the first time in years, he felt truly free—not just from the walls of the prison, but from the weight he'd carried for so long.

Instructional Break: Freedom Within and Without

Reflection Questions:

• What does freedom mean to you—physically, emotionally, and mentally?

• What are three small steps you can take today to align with the person you want to become?

• How can you create a ritual or practice to mark new beginnings in your life?

Write these reflections in the space provided or in a journal. Focus on the creation rather than the pain.

Practice: A Ritual for New Beginnings

1. Find a quiet space where you feel calm and grounded.

2. Write down three intentions for this new chapter of your life.

3. Take a deep breath and say aloud: *"I release the past. I step into my future with strength and grace."*

4. Close your eyes for a moment of gratitude, then move forward with your day.

Suggested Readings:

1. Jeremiah 29:11 (Bible): Reflect on the promise of hope and a future.

2. Bhagavad-Gita: Explore themes of stepping into purpose and destiny.

3. Tao Te Ching (Verse 64): Consider the importance of small steps in creating great change.

Part Five
Tool For Life

Every journey needs a toolkit—a set of practices, principles, and habits that keep you grounded as you navigate life's challenges. Part 5 serves as a guide, providing practical tools to help you integrate the lessons from this book into your daily life.

CHAPTER 13
PRACTICES FOR TRANSFORMATION

Ethan sat at the small desk in his apartment, a stack of notebooks and loose papers spread out before him. It had been six months since his release, and life on the outside had been both everything he'd hoped for and nothing he could have imagined.

There were days when the weight of the world felt heavier than ever—when the old habits and thoughts tried to claw their way back in. But there were also days when he felt unstoppable, like the man he'd fought so hard to become was finally stepping into his full power.

What had carried him through, more than anything, were the practices Marcus had taught him—the tools that had grounded him in the hardest moments, the routines that reminded him of who he was and who he wanted to be.

Now, as he flipped through his notebooks, Ethan realized he had created something more than just a personal toolkit. He had created a way of living, a path that could guide not just him, but anyone who was ready to do the work.

The Power of Daily Practice

Ethan remembered something Marcus had said to him early on:

> "The small things you do every day are what change your life."

At the time, it had felt like an impossible task—how could something as simple as writing in a notebook or taking a deep breath really make a difference? But now, he understood.

It wasn't the grand gestures that mattered. It was the quiet moments of intention, the choices no one else saw.

The Toolkit for Transformation

Ethan began to organize his notes, pulling together the practices that had been most meaningful in his journey. Each one felt like a piece of the puzzle, a step on the path to becoming the man he wanted to be.

1. Breath work for Grounding and Calm

• *Inhale deeply for 4 counts, hold for 4 counts, and exhale slowly for 6 counts.*

• This simple practice had carried Ethan through countless moments of doubt and fear, helping him center himself and stay present.

. . .

2. Journaling for Self-Reflection

- Questions Marcus had shared, like *"What am I pretending not to know?"* and *"What kind of man do I want to be today?"* became the foundation of Ethan's journaling practice.

- Writing wasn't about finding the right answers—it was about being honest with himself and giving his thoughts a place to land.

3. Visualization for Strength and Confidence

- Ethan often returned to the image of the lion Marcus had introduced to him—the steady gaze, the quiet strength.

- Before big decisions or challenging moments, he would close his eyes and picture himself embodying that same energy.

4. Meditation for Emotional Balance

- Sitting in silence, focusing on his breath or a single word like *acceptance* or *strength*, had helped Ethan process emotions that once felt overwhelming.

5. Movement for Energy and Focus

• Simple yoga poses like Warrior II and Tree Pose had become part of Ethan's morning routine, grounding him in his body and preparing him for the day ahead.

6. Acts of Service for Connection

• Ethan had found that helping others—whether it was mentoring someone at work or simply listening to a friend—brought a sense of purpose and fulfillment he hadn't expected.

Passing the Torch

As Ethan compiled these practices, he realized he wasn't just creating a guide for himself. He was creating something he could share—a way to help others find their own path, just as Marcus had helped him.

He thought back to something Marcus had told him during one of their last conversations: *"The greatest legacy you can leave is the tools to help someone else heal."*

Ethan smiled, closing his notebook. He wasn't perfect, and he never would be. But he had something to offer, and for the first time in his life, he felt ready to give it.

∽

Chapter 13

Instructional Break: Your Personal Toolkit

Reflection Questions:

• What practices or routines have helped you feel grounded and focused?

• Which of Ethan's tools resonates with you the most?

• How can you begin to integrate one small, meaningful practice into your daily life?

Write these reflections in the space provided or in a journal. Focus on the lessons rather than the pain.

Practice: Building Your Toolkit

1. Start Small: Choose one practice from the list above to try today.

2. Stay Consistent: Commit to it for one week, noticing how it impacts your mindset and energy.

3. Expand: Gradually add more tools to your routine as you feel ready.

Suggested Readings:

1. Psalm 23 (Bible): Reflect on the themes of guidance and restoration.

2. Bhagavad-Gita: Explore the teachings on self-discipline and balance.

3. Tao Te Ching (Verse 44): Consider the importance of simplicity and focus in building a meaningful life.

Chapter 14
The King's Reflection

As this journey comes to a close, it's important to remember that this book isn't just a story. It's a guide born from the belief that transformation is possible for anyone willing to do the work. Ethan's story is fictional, but his struggles, his victories, and the tools he used to rebuild his life are deeply real.

This book was created for those who may not have access to a mentor or guide in their lives—a way to provide the wisdom and support that might otherwise feel out of reach. It's a reflection of the challenges so many of us face, especially when life feels overwhelming and the path forward seems unclear.

The lessons woven throughout these chapters are not tied to one belief system or way of thinking. Instead, they draw from the rich tapestry of wisdom found in texts like the *Bhagavad-Gita*, the *Tao Te Ching*, the Bible, and beyond. They also incorporate modern practices like mindfulness, breath work, and somatic healing—accessible tools that can guide anyone, anywhere, toward growth and self-mastery.

. . .

The Purpose of This Work

The idea for *Mentoring the Kings* was born from a deep understanding that many people feel trapped—by their circumstances, their pasts, or their own minds. This book was created to offer a way out, to show that even in the darkest moments, there is a path forward.

It is for those who, like Ethan, may feel stuck or defeated but still carry a spark of hope, however small. It is for those who are ready to ask the hard questions, face the uncomfortable truths, and take the first steps toward change.

This book is also a testament to the power of mentorship. Whether it's through a personal relationship like Ethan and Marcus's, or through the guidance of a book like this one, mentorship has the ability to transform lives.

The King in You

As you close this book, remember that the tools and practices shared here are not meant to stay on the page. They are meant to be lived, tried, and adapted to your unique journey. The story of Ethan is, in many ways, the story of all of us—our struggles, our resilience, and our ability to rise.

The "king" Marcus spoke of isn't about status or perfection. It's about stepping into your power, owning your choices, and leading your life with strength and integrity. That king lives in each of us, waiting to be awakened.

A Final Invitation

The journey doesn't end here. It begins now, with you.

Take what resonates from these pages and let it guide you. Ask yourself the questions Marcus asked Ethan. Practice the tools, reflect on the lessons, and keep moving forward—even when it feels hard.

Because just like Ethan, you are capable of transformation. You are worthy of healing. And you are more powerful than you realize.

Work Cited

The Holy Bible: Amplified Version: https://sermoncentral.com/bible/amplified-bible-amp

The Holy Bible: New International Version: https://www.thenivbible.com/

The Holy Bible: King James Version": https://www.kingjamesbibleonline.org/

Bhagavad-Gita: https://www.holy-bhagavad-gita.org/

Tao Te Ching: https://daoism.org/the-tao-te-ching/

The Alchemist: https://archive.org/details/alchemist0000coel_w2i7

The Quran: https://quran.com/

The Story of Buddha: https://www.biography.com/religious-figures/buddha

www.ingramcontent.com/pod-product-compliance
Lightning Source LLC
Chambersburg PA
CBHW071224160426
43196CB00012B/2409